Data Analytics for Beginners

A Beginner's Guide to Learn and Master Data Analytics

ROBERT J. WOZ

© **Copyright 2017 by Robert J. Woz- All rights reserved.**

The following eBook is reproduced below with the goal of providing information that is as accurate and reliable as possible. The Publication is sold with the idea that the publisher is not required to render accounting, officially permitted, or otherwise, qualified services. Professionals should be consulted as needed prior to undertaking any of the action endorsed herein.

This declaration is deemed fair and valid by both the American Bar Association and the Committee of Publishers Association and is legally binding throughout the United States.

Furthermore, the transmission, duplication or reproduction of any of the following work including specific information will be considered an illegal act irrespective of if it is done electronically or in print. This extends to creating a secondary or tertiary copy of the work or a recorded copy and is only allowed with express written consent from the Publisher. All additional right reserved.

The information in the following pages is broadly considered to be a truthful and accurate account of facts and as such any inattention, use or misuse of the information in question by the reader will render any resulting actions solely under their purview. There are no scenarios in which the publisher or the original author of this work can be in any fashion deemed liable for any hardship or damages that may befall them after undertaking information described herein.

Additionally, the information in the following pages is intended only for informational purposes and should thus be thought of as universal. As befitting its nature, it is presented without assurance regarding its prolonged validity or interim quality. Trademarks that are mentioned are done without written consent and can in no way be considered an endorsement from the trademark holder.

Table of Contents

Introduction 5
Chapter 1: How to Think About Data? 7
Chapter 2: Data Analysis Introduction 14
Chapter 3: What Is Data Mining? 22
Chapter 4: Data Mining Functionalities 46
Chapter 5: Basics of Big Data Analytics 59
Chapter 6: Methods of Big Data Analytics 70
Chapter 7: Statistical Methods of Big Data Analytics 105
Conclusion 110

Introduction

Congratulations for downloading ***Data Analytics for Beginners:*** *A Beginner's Guide to Learn and Master Data Analytics* and thank you for doing so. There is a lot of data that is being processed every second in companies and even in our daily lives. Companies should be prepared to learn basic procedures and methods that can help to analyze these data to prepare the business for the present and the future.

This eBook has been created to help you to prepare data for different kinds of use. You will be able to unlock the possibilities that the data you collect have for your business. Some information is a bit complex, but we have made it easy for you to understand by using steps to ease the learning curve. We have listed simple data analysis tools to help you understand your data by following simple procedures. The purpose of this book is to prepare you with simple frameworks for you to think about, work with and benefit from, to finally use your data for various purposes.

The first part of this book introduces you to the definitions of data and the different types of data and data strategies. The second chapter introduces you to data analysis and how you can measure the data you are collecting. The third chapter goes ahead to explain you to what is referred to as data mining. In this section, we take you through the steps of how data that is useful is extracted from the large sets of data. We take you through the processes and even the systems that will help you in extracting different kinds of information.

In chapter four, we are going to take you through the functionalities of data analysis. This is where we show you how data is characterized differently to identify patterns in it which helps to make sense of data that is being collected, equipping you to make better business decisions.

In chapter five, we are going to look at the basics of data analytics. This involves the traditional way of data analysis and the current ways in which data is being analyzed. We intend to show you how the different data analysis procedures are being used as powerful and effective tools to understand data.

There are plenty of books on this subject on the market, thanks again for choosing this one! Every effort was made to ensure it is full of as much useful information as possible; please enjoy!

Chapter 1: How to Think About Data?

According to the Webster Dictionary of 1973, data refers to information that is factual; it is used to discuss, reason and calculate. It can also be defined as information that is needed for analysis. This information can be in numerical form, ready to be processed and transmitted digitally.

From the definitions we have listed above, we can practically define data as characters, numbers, images or any kind of recording, that is in a format that can be assessed for a decision on an action to be arrived at on. There is a belief that goes around that data that stands alone does not have any meaning, and it only gets its meaning when it is interpreted to become information. When data is examined closely, some patterns can be identified, which can later be used as knowledge.

When you look at disciplines such as nutrition, public health, education, management and nursing, it is evident that the quantity and quality of data, be it descriptive or statistical, is required to have baselines, get actions that are effective, set targets and goals, evaluate impacts and monitor progress.

Before presentation and interpretation of information, there have to be procedures for collecting and filtering data. For instance, if you have the number 2146, that is just a number but is basically a raw number without meaning. Just like cabbage or crop that is picked from the farm is raw and not yet prepared. That's how we view data as a raw material that has the potential of becoming information.

During data collection, it is important to identify the best data to collect. One needs to understand that there are several forms by which data can be collected. These forms include pictures, numbers, articles, tweets, words, and maps. When you try to look at the best form of data collection, the concept of quantitative and qualitative approach is brought up, which can lead to a more difficult program planning. It is at times difficult to come to a conclusion on the qualitative and quantitative data differences since the minds of many people the disparity between the two is based on the notion that one is preferred over the other.

Types of Data

Even though there has been a huge debate over the advantages and disadvantage of quantitative data and quantitative data, we need both types of data to have a high-quality program. There are instances that a qualitative approach will be preferred over quantitative data and vice versa. The thing is that both approaches have differing logics and strengths which address different purposes and questions. It is important to know that there are times when having both worlds make total sense. These situations will prove that combining these approaches will tackle a question and allow for better decisions to be made.

Qualitative Data

If data is represented in a narrative or verbal format, we describe it as qualitative data. Focus groups, questionnaires that are open ended, interviews and other situations that are less structured are how this types of data are collected. A simpler way of looking at data that is qualitative is thinking of words as a way of qualitative data presentation.

Quantitative data

This is data expressed in the form of numeric, where numerical values are either small or large. Values that are numerical may respond to a label or specific category.

- Contrasting types of data
- Qualitative data
- Newspaper articles
- Advisory group minutes
- Logs of Social service
- Agreements of family partnerships
- Minutes for the policy council

Qualitative data

- Tracking system for a child's performance
- Tracking system for health data

Mixed Data

Transaction and enrollment records survey which includes parents, teachers, farmers.

Data strategies

Different strategies of qualitative and quantitative data analyses can provide a data analyst with a way of approaching data in an organized way. This allows the data analyst to form a sequence of different processes, which can be used. We are going to offer several quantitative analysis strategies that can be considered as one work while developing skills in the analysis of data; we are also going to include reasons as to why this strategy should be considered.

Strategy: Data visualization

This involves the creation of a picture or graphic data display. This is with the intention of starting the process of analysis; or aid to reporting or findings representation.

Strategy: Analyses that is Exploratory

This involves looking at data to describe what is happening, by creating a baseline for the analysis of the future.

Strategy: Use of Trends

This involves looking at collected data that occurs at different times, with the intention of identifying and estimating change.

Strategy: estimation

This involves the use of real data values that can predict the future value. This is with the aim of countering boredom after mastering all other strategies listed above.

Data Visualization

This means the creation of a visualized display of data. This is not ideally an analysis, nor is it a substitute for analysis. However, data visualization can be used as a start before data analysis.

Analysis that is Exploratory

This entails going through data that has low levels of knowledge about a certain indicator like the 1st and 2nd language acquisition. A relationship between an indicator and its cause can also be included.

Estimation

When working with qualitative or quantitative data, these procedures can occur. The use of data about poverty levels can be combined with interviews from providers who serve families who are low-income earners to assist in determining families in the area that are eligible for income. Planning for the future can be assisted by estimation. Forecasting quantities closely related to eligible families and children, demographic characteristics and social services, can work well using estimation. Ideally, estimation refers to the combination of info that originates from various sources of data to project information that is not available in a singular source.

Trend Analysis

The basic goal of trend analysis is the overview of data over some time. For instance, to discover if a certain indicator like the no. Of children who have disabilities has decreased or increased over time, and if that is the case, how fast or slow as the decrease or increase occurred. One can compare two different time periods. This kind of analysis of trends is conducted to assess the indicator's level before and after a particular event.

Chapter 2: Data Analysis Introduction

TERM	EXPLANATION
Code	An important category that is needed by a data analyst or data scientist for the analysis. It is a technique that is used to label information pieces that are important and that are in a narrative.
Analysis	An investigation of individual parts of a subject and its relations in making up the whole subject. It can also be a separation of a subject to its individual parts to study its parts and its relations.
Correlation	This is a relation that is statistical between variables such that changes that are systemic in a variable's value are accompanied by changes that are systemic in the other. It is a statistic that closely

	represents two variables that co-vary from -1 to 0 to +1.
Denominator	a fraction's divisor
Data	Facts that are collected where conclusions can be drawn
Estimation	The judgement of somebody or something. A calculation that is an approximation of quantity or degree
Interpretation	This is an explanation of a subject that is not obvious at first
Numerator	A fraction's dividend

Methods and Data Procedures

Different procedures exist that may be used in quantitative data analysis. The two basic types include:

- Variance Measures
- Summary measures

Variance Measures

Questions to be considered in variance measurement

- What are the differences between each person in a group?
- What is the difference between scores?
- What are the possible outcomes?

Instances of variance measures

20 participants rate a session by the use of a survey

The training session was beneficial:

Strongly Disagree   Disagree

_____   _____

Agree   Strongly Agree

_____   _____

The result

Strongly Disagree   Disagree

45	3
Agree	Strongly Agree
1	1

In this instance the variance is low. Participants strongly disagreed, and we can see that they felt the training was not beneficial to them

The importance of variance measurement is that it shows the differences. This is indicated, one can look for an explanation and counter check its importance.

Summary Measures

The questions that need to be looked into include:

- What is the average value?
- At what point does data converge?
- Where is the group's center?

Kinds of Summary Measures

Mean is the average of arithmetic scores

Example of scores: 87, 65, 34, 97, 25,

Mean = 61.6

Median is the score that is in the middle

Examples of scores 87, 65, 34, 97, 25, 64, 51

Median 97

Mode is the largest no of scores.

Example of scores 87, 87, 65, 34, 97, 25,

Mode is 87.

Qualitative Data Analysis

Some ways can be used to analyze qualitative data. A narrative analysis that uses interviews and questionnaires can be used.

In the instance below, we are going to see a transcript that can be used as a data source.

Data Analytics for Beginners

(Family one – husband)
OK, well, me first, before anything, I came here because of the poverty, do you understand me? And for a good quality of life, in my country not so much thinking about myself but about my smaller sisters so that they can have a better education considering that I did not have any, and another reason was in my country there are no good jobs, and very little work. They pay you very little and you never leave the poverty and another reason is that my father had two brothers that were already here and I thought that the more of us that are here the better that everybody could help each other out and it would be easier to get ahead with our younger sisters.

(Family one – wife)
The same to help my parents I came and I would send money and then my brother came and then the same.

(Family one – husband)
Because in her case, she or better yet sometimes us (in our situation) because we were the eldest, we were men but in her case the eldest are women, and the ones that were going to work, theoretically to help the parents the most were the youngest.

(Family one-wife)
My dad was already here when I came, he was here, mi mother was in Mexico, my dad stayed here for some time and than he went to Mexico.

(Family one-husband)
More than anything, my parents for example they are that type of people that support you no they never stop, for example your dreams do not become reality they always try that if you decide, you know who you are, and they always let us what we wanted better yet things that they showed us and that were good we would do them and they always tried to better us.

The 1st step is qualitative data analysis which allows the arrangement of data in a format that is manageable, leading to the facilitation of the process of assigning themes and codes to the transcript sections.

Text	Code	Theme
OK, well, me first, before anything, I came here because of the poverty, do you understand me?	Poverty	Purpose for migration
And for a good quality of life, in my country not so much thinking about myself but about my smaller sisters so that they can have a better education considering that I did not have any	Family Life Better education	Purpose for migration/ family
and another reason was in my country there are no good jobs, and very little work.	Work	Purpose for migration

With an established theme, the number of times the theme is identified has to be counted. At this particular time, the themes can be placed in their frequency.

Theme	Frequency	Strength	Barrier
Purpose for migration	2		
Purpose for migration/ family	1		

After utilizing the format above to manage the data narrative, you may want to know if the theme is a barrier or strength. The theme's identification as a barrier or a strength helps in the prioritization and planning.

Chapter 3: What Is Data Mining?

What Is Data Mining

In a simple definition, data mining is the extraction of information from a group of data. By definition, it is a misnomer. You can relate it with gold-mining in sand or rocks – we refer to this process as gold mining and not sand or rock mining. Therefore, data mining should be seen as knowledge mining because we are digging information from data. The term knowledge mining is somehow long, and it may not reflect mining from data. Mining is the process that locates a set of nuggets from raw material. Therefore, it is a misnomer that has a different meaning to mining of data; like data knowledge mining, analysis of patterns, extraction of knowledge, data dredging and data archaeology.

There is also a tendency to relate data mining to Knowledge Discovery from Data (KDD). Other people view mining of data as an important step in knowledge discovery. There is a sequence of iterative steps that are highlighted below:

1. Data cleaning - removal of data that is inconsistent and noise

2. Integration of data - where several sources of data can be combined.

3. Selection of data - data that is relevant to the task analysis is gotten from the database.

4. Transformation of data - data is consolidated or transformed in a manner that is appropriate for mining, by undertaking aggregate or summary of operations.

5. Data mining - is a process where methods that are intelligent are used to extract patterns of data.

6. Evaluation of patterns - to determine interesting patterns that represent knowledge that underlies some measures.

7. Presentation of knowledge - visualization and techniques of the presentation of knowledge help to show the user what has been mined.

Steps 1 to 4 are different kinds of preprocessing of data, where there is a preparation of mining data. The knowledge base or the user may interact with this steps of data mining. The user is presented with interesting patterns that can be stored in the knowledge base as knowledge. When this view is considered, data mining is a single step in the whole process, even though it is a vital one, since it shows patterns that have been hidden. We need to understand that data mining is a piece of the whole process of knowledge discovery. However, in different industries like in media and database research, data mining is popularly compared to KDD. We, therefore, look at data mining as a process of the knowledge discovery from groups of data that are large and kept in data-warehouses, databases, and in other storage areas of information.

Considering this perspective, the structure of a general system of mining data may share the parts that follow:

Data warehouse, database, World Wide Web, other repositories of information

This includes one or several sets of databases, spreadsheets, data warehouses, or other repositories. Data integration and data cleaning techniques may be done on the data.

Data warehouse server of database

The data warehouse or database is responsible in data fetching that is relevant, based on the request of the data mining of the user.

Knowledge base

This is the knowledge that is a domain that guides the search or evaluation of the discovered patterns. The knowledge becomes useful in the organization of attributes or value attributes at various abstraction levels. Knowledge like the beliefs of users that may help to assess the interesting nature of a pattern based on its unexpectedness may be added.

Engine of data mining

It is an essential component of the system of data mining, and it consists of functional modules for tasks like characterization, correlation analysis, association, prediction, classification, cluster analysis, evolution analysis and outlier analysis.

Pattern evaluation module

This component employs measures and interacts with modules of data mining to focus search onto interesting patterns. Thresholds of interesting nature may be used to filter patterns that have been discovered. On the other side, the module of pattern evaluation may be placed in the module of mining, which relies on the data mining method that is implemented. To achieve efficient mining of data, it is advisable to push evaluation of the pattern deep into the process of mining to restrict the interesting patterns search.

User Interface

It is the communication face module between the system of data mining and the user. It allows someone to make queries to the system as a way of mining data, by providing info that will help in the search and the exploration of that heavily depends on the results that are produced intermediately during the mining of data. Additionally, the user of the system is allowed to search for the data structures and mined patterns that are evaluated, or schemas and visualization of different forms of patterns of data warehouse and the database.

Looking at the data warehouse angle, data mining can be looked at as an advanced online Analytical Processing stage (OLAP). But data mining extends further than the scope of processing analytically, summarized systems in a data warehouse, by adding high-level analytical techniques of data.

Even though various systems of data mining are available to users, not all systems can provide good services when it comes to mining of data. An analytical tool for data that does not involve large data sets should be categorized either as a system of machine learning, a tool for analyzing data statistically, or a prototype of a system that is being tested. A system which can retrieve data, including the location of summed values, or one that can deduce answering queries in databases that are large, would be categorized as a database system, deductive database system, and info retrieval system.

Integration of different techniques from different disciplines, like data warehousing, machine learning, statistics, pattern recognition, high-performance computing, signal processing, information retrieval, data visualization, neural networks, temporal; data analysis and image processing are all involved in data mining.

To have a scalable algorithm, it should have a running time that grows linearly, proportionate to the data size, provided the resource available like disk space and main memory. When data mining is done, regularities, the knowledge that is interesting, information that is advanced can be gotten from storage spaces and searched from every angle possible. The knowledge that is discovered can be used to make decisions, in information management, process control and processing of queries. This brings us to the fact that data mining is an important frontier in information systems and database, and it is a promising development in I.T.

What Type of Data Is Mined?

We shall look at several data repositories where mining can be done. Ideally, data mining can be done in any repository of data, as well as in data streams and data that is transient. The scope of examination of repositories so data includes data warehouses, relational databases, database systems that are advanced, data streams, the WWW and flat files. When you look at high-level database systems, it includes relational databases that are object oriented and databases that are inclined to applications like spatial, text, multimedia and time-series databases. Issues and techniques in mining may be different when it comes to the storage systems.

We are going to provide basic knowledge of information systems in each category of a depository that is listed.

1. Relational Databases

A DBMS which is what we call a database management system comprises of an interrelated data that is called a database, and a set of software that helps in the management of data. The programs that are used involve mechanisms for data structure definition, data storage, shared, concurrent and distributed access to data. The software system also provides the security and consistency of information that is stored, despite the crashes of the system or unauthorized access attempts.

In a relational database, tables are the main components, and each component has a unique name. Each table has fields and columns that store sets of data in rows. Each row represents an item that is identified by the use of a primary key and a description of a values attribute. A semantic data model like an Entity Relationship model is used in relational databases. An ER data model represents a database as a set of entities and relationships that is in them.

Consider an example below:

A relational database for a company Q. The company Q is described by tables that are relational in nature: the table comprises of following relation branch, customer, employee, and item.

Customer consists of attributes that include a customer who is uniquely identified by an id number, customer ID, customer name, age, address, employment type, category, income, etc.

Each relation employee, item, branch consists of some attributes that describe properties.

Tables can represent relationships among tables that are relational. For instance, purchases table (this table has customer who has purchased some items, it creates a sale transaction that an employee handles), items sold table (list items that have been sold after a transaction has been made, as works at table (includes where the employee works in company Q's branch)

Database queries can access relational data using a query language that is relational like SQL or using graphical user interface (GUI). When using a GUI, a user uses a menu. An example is to indicate attributes that a query should have and the attribute's constraints. Transformation to a query is done to relational operations, like join, projection, and selection, and it is then optimized to process efficiently. Using a query gives you the chance of removing data subsets.

As a data analyst at company Q, you can ask the database several things using relational queries. For instance, you can also include aggregate function in the relational language. These functions include avg, sum, max, count, and min; you would ask something like "I need to see the total sales for the last two months by branch?" or "Who had the highest sales in the last month?"

When mining data in relational databases, you can go an extra mile into searching data patterns or trends. For instance, systems of data mining can analyze the data of the customer to form a credit risk prediction for each new customer depending on their age and income. Systems of data mining can identify deviations, like items whose sales go beyond the expected, compared to sales of the previous year. These kinds of deviations can be investigated. Relational databases are commonly available as rich repositories of information, and thus they are a major data form when we are studying data mining.

2. Data Warehouses

If company Q is an international company, that has a presence in different countries around the world; each station in each country has its own database. The president of company Q then requests for an analysis of the company's sales in each station or branch, for each item sold in the second quarter. It is a difficult task because the data that is relevant is spread out in different databases that are physically placed in different sites.

If company Q owned one data warehouse, then it would not be such an uphill task. When you collect information from different sources and store it in one storage facility under a schema on a site, then it is called - data warehouse. Data warehouses are made through data transformation, data cleaning, data transformation, data refreshing that is on a periodic time scale and data loading.

To help in the making of decisions, the data warehouse data is organized very well on subjects that are specific, like the item, the customer, and the supplier. Historical information that goes as far as ten years stored as the summary is made available to the user. For instance, instead of documenting each transaction's detail, a warehouse of the data stores the summary of the transaction's history of each item type for each region's sales.

A multidimensional data structure models a data warehouse, where the dimension corresponds to a group of attributes that are found in the schema and summed measure is stored in a storage cell. These include sales amount and count. The data warehouse's real structure may be either a multidimensional data cube or a relational data store. A multidimensional data view is provided by a data cube which allows early computation and access to data that is summarized fast.

3. Transactional Database

The type of database comprises of a file that has a record that stands for a transaction. The transaction has an identification number of a transaction (trans_id) that is unique and an items list that makes the transaction.

A database that is transactional may include additional tables related to it, which contains more details about the sale that includes the transaction date, customer ID, sales person number and the branch/station where the transaction happened, etc.

4. Advanced Applications and Information Systems

Database systems that are relational are being used broadly in different applications in business. Since database technology has progressed over the years, all kinds of intelligent data systems and data sets have come up, and they are continuously improved or upgraded to manage the requirements of the application in today's business environment.

The new applications of database include: spatial data (maps) handling, engineering data design (like building designs, integrated circuits, or system components), multimedia and hypertext (which include image, text, audio and video data), real time data (like stock exchange data and historical records), stream data (like video sensor and surveillance data, where there is data flows in and out of streams), and the WWW (a large information repository that is distributed and accessible through the internet). These applications need data structures that are efficient and scalable to handle object structures that are complex; records of variable length; unstructured and semi structured data; spatiotemporal, text, database schemas that have dynamic changes and complex structures and multimedia data.

With these needs in mind, database systems that are advanced and specific application oriented databases have been created. This comprises of object-related databases, time oriented and temporal databases, spatiotemporal and spatial databases, legacy and heterogeneous databases, multimedia and text databases, information systems that are globally based and management systems for data streams.

While these kinds of databases which are highly sophisticated need efficient storage, retrieval, update when it comes to complex data, they provide ideal grounds and raise issues related to the implementation and research of data mining.

5. Databases That Are Object Related

These databases consist of a data model that is object related. This type of data model stretches the relational model by the use of a data type that is rich for object orientation and handling of objects that are complex. Since most complex database applications have to manage sophisticated structures and objects, object related databases are now becoming popular in applications and industry.

Data model that is object related adopts object-oriented databases' concepts, where, every entity is identified as a singular object. If we look at company Q, objects are identified as customers, items or employees. An object's code and data are encapsulated to one unit. The following are associated with one object:

- Variables that are object descriptive. This relates to attributes in relational models and relationships of entities.

- Messages that an object uses to communicate with different objects, or with the database system.

- Methods that hold the code for message implementation. When the message is received, the method responds to a value. For example, get photo (employee) message retrieves and displays the photo of an employee.

Objects are grouped according to their properties to form what is called - object class. One class has an object's instance. Object classes are organized into hierarchy subclasses for each class to represent properties common to objects in the class. For example, a class employee can have variables such as address, name, and date of birth. Assume that the salesperson class inherits all the variables that are in the superclass of the employee. Additionally, it has variables that specifically pertain to a salesperson. This type of class inheritance is an advantage to sharing of information.

For object-relational system in data mining, there have to be set techniques that can be used in the management of object structures that are complex, data types that are complex, subclass & class hierarchies, methods & procedures and property inheritance.

6. Sequence, Temporal, And Time-Series Databases

A temporal database keeps relational data which comprise of attributes that are time-related. These attributes normally include some time stamps which have different semantics.

A database that is sequential stores sequences of events that are ordered with or without time. Instances include streams of web links, biological sequences, and customer shopping sequences.

A database that is referred to as time series stores value sequences that are gained, or events that are gained, over time measurements that are repeated. (for instance, weekly, daily, hourly). Instances comprise data that is gathered from inventory control, stock exchange, and natural phenomena observation.

Techniques of data mining can be used to search the characteristics of the evolution of objects, or the trend changes of objects in a database. This kind of information can be used in making decisions and planning of strategy. For example, banking data mining may help in the bank teller scheduling depending on the volume of customers. Data mined in stock exchange can be used in trend identification that might help in planning for investments strategically (e.g., the appropriate time to buy a company Q stock.) Several granularities can be defined for such kind of analyses. For instance, decomposition of time can be done according to the academic years, fiscal or calendar years. The years can be further broken down into months and quarters.

7. Spatiotemporal and Spatial Databases

Databases that are spatial have information that is spatial related. For instance, maps or geographic databases, computer graphics aided databases, (VLSI) very large-scale integration, satellite, medical and image databases. Data that is spatial can be in what is referred to as raster format. This consists of a number of dimensions; bit maps. An instance is a 2-Dimensional satellite image that can be in the form of raster data, having the pixels register rainfall in an area. Vector format can also be a representation of maps, where bridges, roads, lakes, and buildings are identified using overlay or unions of constructs of basic geometry, like points, polygons, lines and partitions & networks formed by these parts.

There are several applications for geographic databases, which range from ecology and forestry planning to public service info that regards the telephone and electric cable locations, sewage and pipes sewage systems. Additionally, geographic databases currently exist in vehicle dispatching & navigation systems. An instance of this is taxis that store a map of a city with info that regards to 1-way streets; routes suggested that help people move from one point to the next during a rush hour is, and the location of the hospitals and restaurant, and each drivers' location.

Question: How can data mining take place on spatial databases?

Patterns may be uncovered by data mining that describes the house's characteristics that are close to the specific location, like a park. Some patterns may make a description of the mountain area climate in different altitudes, or they may make a description of changes in modern poverty trends that are based on distances of cities from the highways that are well known. Spatial objects relationships can be looked into, to realize the object's subsets that are spatially associated or auto-correlated. Outliers and clusters can be identified as analysis of spatial clusters. Additionally, a classification that is regarded as spatial can be done to create prediction models, by the right spatial objects characteristics. Cubes of spatial data may be created to group data into hierarchies and structures that are multidimensional, where OLAP operations can be done. These operations are like the drill-down and the roll up.

Spatial objects that alter with time and are found in a spatial database are grouped into this database called spatiotemporal database. It is where information that is interesting is mined. For instance, trends of objects on the move may be grouped, identification of moving vehicles can be done, differentiation of a normal flu outbreak from a bioterrorist attack can also be done, based on the disease spread on a geographical location.

8. Multimedia and Text Databases

Text databases contain descriptions of objects in words. These descriptions in words are not keywords that are not that simple; they have paragraphs and long sentences like the specification of products, bug or error reports, warning messages, documents and summary reports. Text databases may be unstructured highly (just like website pages on the internet). A couple of text databases can be semi-structured (e.g., other web pages and messages in email), while they are structured well (like databases of library catalogs). Text databases that have extensive regular structures ideally can use relational databases for implementation.

Question: what can be uncovered using data mining?

When text data is mined, it is possible to uncover general descriptions of the keyword, content association, text, together with clustering text objects behavior. For this to be done, data mining methods that are standard need to relate to techniques for retrieving information and the creation or use of text data specific hierarchies (like thesaurus and dictionaries), as well as classification systems that are discipline-oriented (like biochemistry, economics, law, and medicine).

Multimedia databases record audio, video and image data. These are used in the video-on-demand systems, voice-mail systems, picture retrieval, speech based interfaces and the WWW that can identify spoken input commands. Databases of multimedia must have objects that are large, because of the data objects like videos that need gigabytes for it to be stored. Specific search techniques and storage are needed for this. Audio and video data need the retrieval at a consistent rate in real time to avoid sound and picture gaps and overflows of system buffers, which is known as data that is of continuous media.

When it comes to mining of data that is of a multimedia type, storage and learning techniques have to be combined with methods of mining data that are standard. Ways that are promising include the development of multi-media data cubes.

9. Legacy and Heterogeneous Databases

A legacy database is a group of heterogeneous databases. In heterogeneous databases, there is a set of independent, interconnected databases.

Data Analytics for Beginners

There is communication between components to communicate and provide answers to queries. Objects differ from one database to the other, and this makes it hard when assimilating semantics into one heterogeneous database.

Legacy databases are needed in many enterprises, due to the I.T technological development that includes the application of various operating systems and hardware.

In a legacy database, different data systems, like object-oriented and relational, network, hierarchical, multimedia, file, and spreadsheets combined. The heterogeneous databases use inter-intra networks to communicate with a legacy database.

There is difficulty in exchange for information across databases because precise transformation rules will be required between representation, considering the semantic which is diverse. For instance, the information exchanging regarding the academic performance of students who are in different schools. Different computer systems may be used by different schools, including different grading systems and curriculum systems.

10. Data streams

Current systems generate and analyze different kinds of data called data stream, where data flows in and out of the window dynamically. The following unique features are identifiable in a data stream:

- Volume that is infinitely huge
- Fixed in and out flow
- A few scans allowed
- Important response that is real-time
- Dynamically changing

Examples of data streams include several types of engineering and scientific data, data of time series, data produced in their environment that are dynamic, like power supply, stock exchange, network traffic, video surveillance, monitoring of environment or the weather, telecommunications and web click streams.

Since data streams are not stored in any data repository, efficient and effective management and data stream analysis poses a great challenge when it comes to research. Discovery of dynamic changes and patterns that are general happen within the data stream, and this is what constitutes data stream mining. For instance, computer network intrusion that is based on message flow anomaly can be identified by data stream clustering, stream models dynamic construction, or frequent patterns comparison; as analysts are interested in advanced abstraction levels. Therefore, multidimensional, multilevel online analysis and mining needs to be done on stream data.

11. World Wide Web

The distributed services of information associated with the WWW, like Google, Yahoo! AltaVista and America Online, provide a service of information that has objects lined for access that is interactive. Users who seek for useful information of shift from one object to the other. Many opportunities and challenges are provided by such systems when it comes to data mining. For instance, understanding patterns of user access will improve the system design and it will also help in deciding on marketing.

Chapter 4: Data Mining Functionalities

There have been different kinds of databases and information storage systems where mining of data can be done. We are going to look at the data patterns that can be mined.

Functionalities of data mining are used to identify the patterns that can be found in tasks of data mining. Generally, tasks in data mining can be categories into two classes: predictive and descriptive

Predictive tasks of mining are done to infer from the data that is current for predictions to be made. Descriptive tasks of mining identify the properties that are common to the data in a database.

There are cases where users will have no clue as to what type of patterns might be interesting in their data, and therefore may like to look in a parallel manner for various patterns. It is recommended that a system capable of data mining which can mine several different patterns to be flexible enough to be used in applications and expectations of different users. Additionally, systems of data mining should uncover patterns at different granularity.

Systems of data mining also should enable users to hint out or zero in the search for patterns that are interesting. Since some patterns are not applicable to all data in a database, trustworthiness is measured, which is associated with the patterns discovered. Functionalities of data mining and the different patterns discovered are looked at in detail below.

Discrimination and Characterization

Concepts and classes can be associated with data. For instance, in company Q, classes that are for sale are printers & computers, and customer concepts have budget Spenders and big Spenders. Concepts and Single classes can be described and summarized in a precise and concise manner. These kinds of descriptions can be gotten from

A) Characterization of data, by summarizing the class data (target class) which is being looked at generally.

B) Discrimination of data, by comparing the target with a set or a singular comparative class (contrasting classes)

C) Both data discrimination of characterization

A general summary of the features or characteristics of a class of data is referred to as data characterization. Data that is related to a class where a user is specified is collected via a query of a database. For instance, the study of the characteristics software products whose sales rose by 15% in the previous year, data that is related to these kinds of products can be gathered by a query of SQL that is executed.

There are some effective characterization and summarization of effective data methods. OLAP data cube based roll-up operation can perform data summarization that is controlled by the user along dimensions that are specified. Data generalization can be done using an induction that is oriented about its attributes, without interaction in step by step basis in characterization. There are various forms of how data characterization needs to be presented; it includes bar & pie charts, multidimensional tables (crosstabs) and pie charts. The descriptions that are produced can be presented as relations that are general or under characteristic rules.

Data Characterization

A system of data mining needs a summary to be shown of the customers' characteristics when they purchase items to a tune of more than $1,000 in a year at company Q. A general profile of the customers that includes their age; employment status can be done. Users should be allowed by the system to get to the dimensions, like on occupation to view customer's dependent on their employment type.

Data Discrimination

This shows the differences in data objects' features for a particular class which has object features that are generally from a set or a singular class that is contrasting. The contrasting and target classes can be specified by a user, and the data objects that are corresponding obtained from queries of a database. For instance, general features may be used to compare products of software that had sales rising by 15% in the year that passed where the sales had dwindled to over 25% within a similar time frame. Discrimination means of data are similar to data characterization methods.

Question: how are the outputs of discrimination descriptions done?

Output presentation forms are the same as those of characteristic descriptions, even though discrimination descriptions need to have measures that are comparative to differentiate the two classes of contrasting and target. Expressed discrimination descriptions are also called discriminant rules.

Data discrimination: A system of data mining needs to compare two groups of customers in company Q, like the ones who purchase computer accessories on a regular basis (more than two months, compared to those who shop on a periodic basis of fewer than four times in one year. The description that is produced makes a customer's comparative profile, like 70% of the customer who shops for computer accessories on a frequent basis are between the ages 20 and 40 and have already attended university, while 50% of the customer purchase computer products on an infrequent basis is either the youth or seniors who have not attended university. When you dig deep into a dimension, like occupation, or when adding dimensions, like income level help to locate more features that are discriminative between two classes.

Correlations, Associations, and Mining Frequent Patterns

Frequent pattern is frequent patterns recurring in data occasionally. Various types of frequent patterns are substructures, item sets & sub-sequences. An item set that is frequent refers to the frequent appearance of items together in a transaction of data set, like milk and bread. Frequently occurring sub-sequence occurs in a pattern where the clients buy a PC, also they purchase a camera and the memory card, this indicates a pattern that is sequentially frequent. Different forms of structures like trees, graphs or lattices can be referred to by substructures, which can be combined with the subsequences or item sets. If there is a frequent occurrence of substructures, is referred to as structured pattern that is frequent. Frequent patterns have mined a discovery of the associations that are interesting and data correlations is achieved.

Example of association analysis:

Let us imagine that you are company Q's marketing manager, and you want to know what is purchased together occasionally in the same transactions. An instance of this type of rule is derived from company Q's relational database

Having X as a customer variable representation. A certainty or confidence of 50% is translated to mean that if a computer is bought by a customer, there is a 50% likelihood that the customer will purchase a software. A support of 1% of the transactions under analysis shows that software and computer were purchased at the same time. This rule of association involves a predicate or one repetitive attribute. Association rules having one predicate are referred to as association rules that are single-dimensional. When there is a drop on the predicate notation, the rule above can be simply written as

$$\textit{"computer} \Rightarrow \textit{software} \ [1\%, 50\%]\textit{"}.$$

If instead, we are given company Q's relational database that related to purchases. Association rules like the one below can be found through a system of data mining.

$$age(X, \text{``20...29''}) \wedge income(X, \text{``20K...29K''}) \Rightarrow buys(X, \text{``CD player''})$$
$$[support = 2\%, confidence = 60\%]$$

The rule above shows that the customers of company Q, 2 percent are between the ages of 20 and 29 who have an income that ranges between 20k and 29k, at the same time purchasing a CD player. A 60 percent chance exists where a customer in between the ages of 20 and 29 can buy a Compact Disk player. We call this an association existing in an attribute or a predicate (An example is. buys, income, and age). Taking their terms in multidimensional databases, where attributes are known as a dimension, the mentioned rule can be perceived as an association of the multidimensional rule. Rules of association that usually are named not to be interesting and cannot quench the confidence threshold that is minimum and the support threshold that is also minimum are not used. There can be more analysis done to check if there are correlations that are interesting statistically better pairs of attribute values which are associated.

Prediction and Classification

Classification is what is referred to as the methods used for discovering models used to describe and differentiate the various concepts and data classes. The intention of using the model is to predict objects with an unknown class label. The model derived is based on training data analysis. (I.e., objects of data with known class labels).

Question: In what way is the derived model presented?

There can be various forms of derived model representation, like classification (IF-THEN) rules, mathematical formulae, neural networks or decision trees.

A decision tree is a tree structure that is a flow chart, which has nodes that tests are denoted on depending on the attributes values, the branches each have a test outcome & the classes or distribution classes are represented as tree leaves. Classification rules can be converted from decision trees.

A neural network is a collection of processing units that are neuron like, having connections that are weighted between units. Other classification methods for model construction are Bayesian naive & k-nearest neighbor classifications and support vector machines.

Since categorical labels like unordered or discrete are predicted by classification, continuous-valued functions are modeled by prediction. It predicts a missing data or data that is unavailable, compared to data values that are numerical. Even though prediction refers to numeric prediction and prediction of the class label, we refer to it as a basically numeric prediction.

Relevance analysis is an attempt to determine attributes that do not add any value to the prediction or classification process.

Regression Analysis

A statistical methodology used to predict numeric, even though other methods are in existence. Prediction also encompasses distribution trend identification that is based on the data that is available.

Example of a prediction and classification:

Assuming you are a sales manager at company Q, and you want to classify several items in the store, with regards to the feedback from the sales campaign: mild, no and good response. You might desire to model these classes dependent on features that are descriptive of the items like price, type, category, and place made. The classification that is resulted should differentiate the classes from one another, do portray a data set that is organized. If the classification that is assumed is achieved, is expressed as a decision tree which may identify price as one of the factors that differentiate objects of a class from another. A decision tree like this one might help in understanding a sales campaign impact and design an effective future campaign.

Assuming that alternatively, the labels can predict categorized response for each item in a store, it is possible for one to predict the revenue of each item that will be generated when the next sale at the company Q will be up; this will be based on the sales data that was there before. We are looking at an example of a prediction that is numeric since the constructed model predicts a function that is an ordered value or of continuous value.

Classification models that can be presented in different forms like

A) IF-then rules

B) Decision trees

C) Neural network

(a)

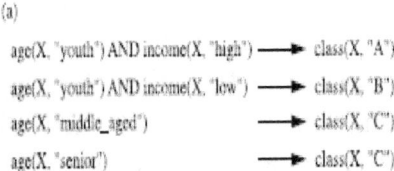

age(X, "youth") AND income(X, "high") ⟶ class(X, "A")
age(X, "youth") AND income(X, "low") ⟶ class(X, "B")
age(X, "middle_aged") ⟶ class(X, "C")
age(X, "senior") ⟶ class(X, "C")

(b)   (c)

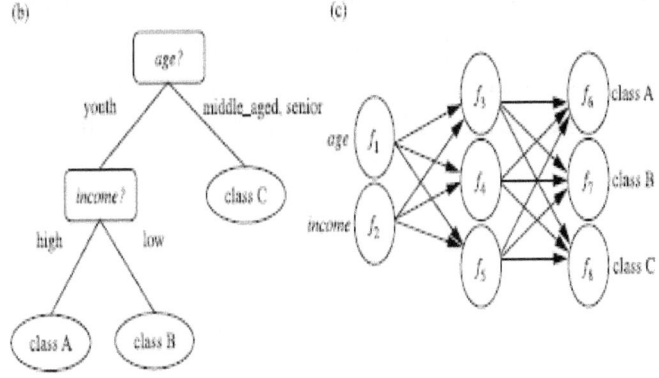

Cluster Analysis

Different from prediction and classification, which analyzes data objects that are class labeled, clustering looks in depth into data objects without class label consulting.

The class labels are not found in training data because they are not identified. Generation of labels can be done through clustering. Grouping of objects solely depends on inter-class maximisation similarity principle and the inter-class minimization similarity. Grouped objects, therefore, are created for objects in a cluster to have similarity compared to the other, but not similar to objects that are in the other clusters. Clusters formed are at this moment looked at objects of one class that are used to obtain the rules. Taxonomy formation can be facilitated by clustering, which is observations of the organization to classes that are in the hierarchy which group events together that are similar.

Chapter 5: Basics of Big Data Analytics

Overview

There is an explosion of data that one has to use over the past decade, and the price of storage of this data has reduced at the same time. Research institutions and private companies get terabytes of data about the interaction of the users in social media, business and from sensors that are located on devices like automobiles and mobile phones. The challenge posed to us is how we can make sense of this ocean of data, and this is what is referred to as big data analytics.

Big data analytics involve the gathering of information from various sources, put them in a way that is available to an analyst who makes sense out of the data and delivers the data products that is useful to the business.

The conversion of large unstructured data that is raw, retrieved from various sources of a data product that is useful to companies is the basis of Big Data Analytics.

Data Life Cycle

To provide a framework to have work organized to achieve clear insights derived from data, we need to think of the process as a cycle that occurs in various stages. The stages are related to each other, and the cycle has similarities that are superficial with more traditional data mining cycle which is the CRISP method.

Crisp Method

CRISP-DM is an abbreviation of Cross Industry Standard Process for Data Mining. It is a process that describes approaches that are common in experts of data mining to handle problems traditionally in data mining in BI. The following illustration shows the major stages of the cycle in CRISP DM method and the interrelations.

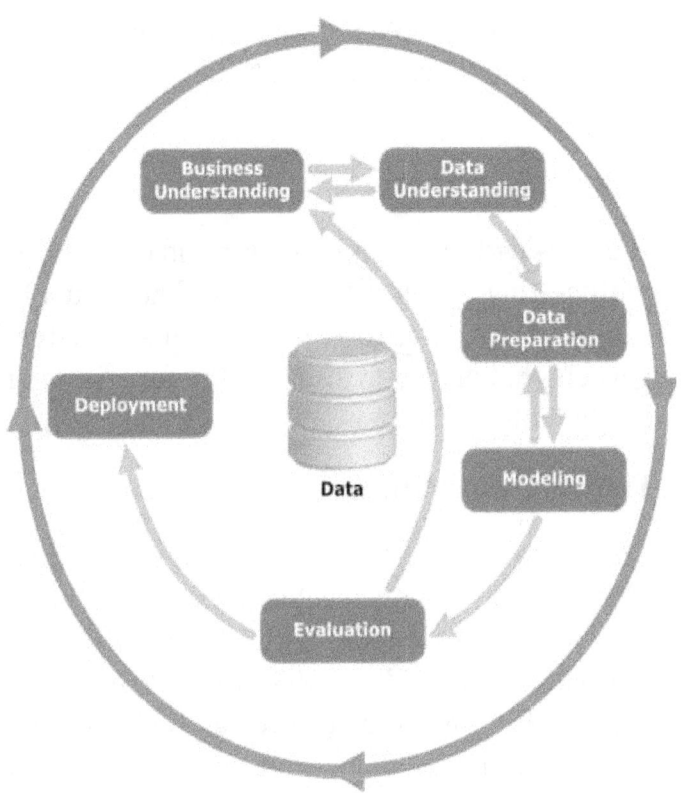

Let us dive into each stage:

Business understanding

This is the first step that focuses on project requirements and objectives understanding from a business angle, and then convert the knowledge to a problem definition in data mining. To achieve this objective, a preliminary plan is devised. A notation standard and a decision model can be used to make a decision model.

Data understanding

It begins with the data collection and goes ahead with getting to know the data, to know quality issues of the data, to realize insights of detect subsets that are interesting for the formation of hidden info hypothesis.

Preparation of data

This stage covers all actions that lead to the final data set that is constructed. Tasks to prepare data tend to be done several times following no particular order. These tasks include attribute, table selection, and record as well as the transformation and data cleaning for tools of modeling.

Modelling

Several techniques of modeling are identified and put into practice, and a calibration of their parameter is done to achieve values that are optimal. Generally, some techniques of the same problem type of data mining are used. Some requirements that are in data form is used in some techniques. Therefore, stepping back is necessary for the phase of data preparation.

Evaluation

A model will have been built at this stage that is of advanced quality, from a perspective of the analysis of data. Before progressing to the model deployment, evaluation of the model is a key with a review of each step executed to build the model, for it to achieve the objectives of the business.

One fundamental objective is the determining of key business issues that have not been considered sufficiently. When the stage comes to an end, a data mining decision will be reached.

Deployment

Model creation is not the final step. Even if the model's purpose is to increase data knowledge, the gained knowledge is prioritized and presented in a useful way to the customer.

This phase can be simple if you consider the requirements at hand. A simple report generation can be achieved, or a repeatable data scoring can be done to make it a complex deployment.

This deployment is majorly done by a customer and not a data analysis. It is important for the customer to understand the action that needs to be carried out to make the created models useful even If the analysis deploys it.

Big data life cycle

In our current business world, the context of big data cannot fully use the approach we have looked at above. The cycle of big data analytics can be described in the stages that follow:

- Business Problem Definition
- Research
- Human resource assessment
- Data acquisition
- Data merging
- Data storage
- Exploratory data analysis
- Data modeling preparation and assessment
- Modelling
- Implementation

Let us look at the stages outlined above in a bit more detail:

Business Problem Definition

This is a common point in traditional BI we looked at and in a life cycle of big data analytics. It is a stage of the big data project that defines the problem and evaluates the potential that it has to the organization. It is obvious to say that the evaluation of the gains to be expected and the project costs have to be identified.

Research

Go through what other companies have done in similar circumstances. The solutions that are convenient for your company needs to be involved, even though adapting other solutions to the resources and requirements of your company is needed. A methodology for stages of the future is defined.

Human Resource Assessment

When the problem is defined, it is reasonable to analyze the staff's capability to complete the project. Teams of traditional BI may not be in the capacity to provide solutions that are optimal in all stages; it should be considered that before the start of a project if there is a need for outsourcing project's part or some more human resource, it should be noted.

Data Acquisition

This is an important part of big data life cycle; it defines the profiles needed to deliver data product that is resulted. Gathering of data is a process that involves the collection of unstructured data from various sources. An instance would involve creating a crawler to get reviews from a website. This involves a text, in different languages which need a lot of time to complete.

Data Munging

For instance, if the data is retrieved from a website, it is stored in a simple format. In the reviews example we just started out on, we can assume that the data is retrieved from various websites where each site has a different data display.

If a data source provides a review in the context of rating, in the beginning, it is possible to map this for the variable that is responsible $y \in \{1,2,3,4\}$. Another source of data provides reviews using an arrow system with one arrow for voting up and the other arrow for voting down. This implies a variable response of $y \in$ (positive, negative}.

To combine the data sources, making a decision has to be done to make the two response representation equivalent. This involves converting a data source representation to the 2nd form when you consider a star as negative and positive as 5 stars. A large allocation of time is used in this process to deliver quality results.

Data storage

When data processing is done, it is often stored in a database. Technologies of big data offer plenty of alternatives in this regard. The most recommended option to Hadoop Five System when it comes to storage which provides a limited version of SQL to users is what is called HIVE Query. It allows analytics to be done like in traditional BI warehouses, from the perspective of the user. Alternative options for storage are Redis, SPARK, and MongoDB.

Traditional warehouses that have been modified are used on a large scale basis. For instance, IB, and Teradata use SQL databases which handle large terabytes of data. MySql and PostgreSQL which are solutions that are open source are also used in large scale applications.

Exploratory data Analysis

When data is cleaned and stored in a manner where insights can be gotten, data exploration is a must. This is done to understand the data. The process that is used is a statistical technique and data plotting. This stage evaluates if the problem definite is feasible.

Data modeling preparation and assessment

Reshaping data that is clean and use of statistical preprocessing is applied to perform imputation of missing values, normalization, Detection of an outlier, feature selection and feature extraction.

Modelling

Some datasets need to have been produced from the previous stage for testing and training; an instance is a predictive model. This stage involves different models and solving a business problem in one hand. Practically, it is desired that the model bring some insight into the business. In the end, the model or set of models is selected to evaluate its performance on a data set that is left out.

Implementation

The developed data product is implemented in the data pipeline of the company. Setting up a scheme of validation is as data is working to track how it is doing. For instance, predictive model implementation can involve model application to data that is new, and when there is a response, the model is evaluated.

Chapter 6: Methods of Big Data Analytics

We are going to look at R programming language which can be downloaded via this link **https://cran.r-project.org**. In case you are using windows, you need to install **rtools** using the same link above, and this link **https://www/rstudio.com.**

R serves as an interface to software that hasbeen developed and compiled using C++ or C, to give one a tool that is interactive to achieve data analysis.

Go to the zip folder bda/part2/R_introduction and file R_introduction.Rproj needs to be opened. ARStudio session will be opened. The 01_vector.Rfile will be opened. The script will need to be opened line by line and the code in the comments to be followed. To learn easily, type the code, which will help you to get familiar with the syntax of R. Comments in R are written using the hash # symbol.

To display the running R code results, the results are commentedin R. you can copy paste the code and try it directly from the book.

```r
# Create a vector of numbers
numbers = c(1, 2, 3, 4, 5)
print(numbers)
# [1] 1 2 3 4 5


# Create a vector of letters
ltrs = c('a', 'b', 'c', 'd', 'e')
# [1] "a" "b" "c" "d" "e"


# Concatenate both
mixed_vec = c(numbers, ltrs)
print(mixed_vec)
# [1] "1" "2" "3" "4" "5" "a" "b" "c" "d" "e"
```

In this code, it is possible for vector creation that has numbers and letters to be achieved. There was no need to tell R the data type we needed. Finally, a vector needs to be created with letters and numbers. The **mixed_vec**vector has changed numbers to characters; this can be observed by how the numbers are displayed in quotes.

We are going to show how data type of different vectors is returned by a function class.

"Interrogation" of an object can be done by a class function.

```r
### Evaluate the data types using class


### One dimensional objects
# Integer vector
num = 1:10
class(num)
# [1] "integer"


# Numeric vector, it has a float, 10.5
num = c(1:10, 10.5)
class(num)
# [1] "numeric"


# Character vector
ltrs = letters[1:10]
class(ltrs)
# [1] "character"


# Factor vector
fac = as.factor(ltrs)
class(fac)
# [1] "factor"
```

Data Analytics for Beginners

2 Dimensional objects are supported by R. In the code below, two of the most important data structures are used. The data.frame and matrix.

```
# Matrix
M = matrix(1:12, ncol=4)
#      [,1] [,2] [,3] [,4]
# [1,]   1    4    7   10
# [2,]   2    5    8   11
# [3,]   3    6    9   12
lM = matrix(letters[1:12], ncol=4)
#      [,1] [,2] [,3] [,4]
# [1,]  "a"  "d"  "g"  "j"
# [2,]  "b"  "e"  "h"  "k"
# [3,]  "c"  "f"  "i"  "l"


# Coerces the numbers to character
# cbind concatenates two matrices (or vectors) in one matrix
cbind(M, lM)
#      [,1] [,2] [,3] [,4]  [,5] [,6] [,7] [,8]
# [1,] "1"  "4"  "7"  "10"  "a"  "d"  "g"  "j"
# [2,] "2"  "5"  "8"  "11"  "b"  "e"  "h"  "k"
# [3,] "3"  "6"  "9"  "12"  "c"  "f"  "i"  "l"


class(M)
# [1] "matrix"
class(lM)
# [1] "matrix"

# data.frame
```

```
# One of the main objects of R, handles different data types in the same
object.

# It is possible to have numeric, character and factor vectors in the same
data.frame


df = data.frame(n=1:5, l=letters[1:5])

df

#   n l

# 1 1 a

# 2 2 b

# 3 3 c

# 4 4 d

# 5 5 e
```

Having different types of data in one object is possible. This is generally how data is shown in databases, APIs data part is character or text vectors and numerals. It is the work of the analyst to determine the data type used to assign and used to correct R data type. In statistics, variables are of the following kinds:

- Ordinal
- Categorical or nominal
- Numeric

In R, the following classes can be available

- Factor
- Ordered Factor
- Numeric - integer

A data type is provided by R for statistical type variables. The ordered factor is not commonly used, but their creation can be done by ordered or by function factor. We are going to look at how problems of section selection of objects are dealt with and how transformations are made on them.

```
# Let's create a data.frame
df = data.frame(numbers=1:26, letters)
head(df)
#     numbers  letters
# 1      1       a
# 2      2       b
# 3      3       c
# 4      4       d
# 5      5       e
# 6      6       f
# str gives the structure of a data.frame, it's a good summary to inspect an object
str(df)
#   'data.frame': 26 obs. of  2 variables:
#   $ numbers: int  1 2 3 4 5 6 7 8 9 10 ...
#   $ letters: Factor w/ 26 levels "a","b","c","d",..: 1 2 3 4 5 6 7 8 9 10 ...

# The latter shows the letters character vector was coerced as a factor.
# This can be explained by the stringsAsFactors = TRUE argumnet in data.frame
# read ?data.frame for more information

class(df)
# [1] "data.frame"


### Indexing
```

Data Analytics for Beginners

```
# Get the first row
df[1, ]
#     numbers  letters
# 1      1        a


# Used for programming normally - returns the output as a list
df[1, , drop = TRUE]
# $numbers
# [1] 1
#
# $letters
# [1] a
# Levels: a b c d e f g h i j k l m n o p q r s t u v w x y z


# Get several rows of the data.frame
df[5:7, ]
#     numbers  letters
# 5      5        e
# 6      6        f
# 7      7        g


### Add one column that mixes the numeric column with the factor column
df$mixed = paste(df$numbers, df$letters, sep='')


str(df)
# 'data.frame':   26 obs. of  3 variables:
# $ numbers: int  1 2 3 4 5 6 7 8 9 10 ...
```

```
# $ letters: Factor w/ 26 levels "a","b","c","d",..: 1 2 3 4 5 6 7 8 9 10 ...
# $ mixed   : chr  "1a" "2b" "3c" "4d" ...


### Get columns
# Get the first column
df[, 1]


# It returns a one dimensional vector with that column


# Get two columns
df2 = df[, 1:2]
head(df2)


#     numbers letters
# 1      1       a
# 2      2       b
# 3      3       c
# 4      4       d
# 5      5       e
# 6      6       f


# Get the first and third columns
df3 = df[, c(1, 3)]
df3[1:3, ]


#     numbers mixed
# 1      1      1a
```

```
# 2      2    2b
# 3      3    3c


### Index columns from their names

names(df)

# [1] "numbers" "letters" "mixed"

# This is the best practice in programming, as many times indeces change, but variable names don't

# We create a variable with the names we want to subset

keep_vars = c("numbers", "mixed")

df4 = df[, keep_vars]


head(df4)

#     numbers mixed
# 1      1    1a
# 2      2    2b
# 3      3    3c
# 4      4    4d
# 5      5    5e
# 6      6    6f


### subset rows and columns

# Keep the first five rows

df5 = df[1:5, keep_vars]

df5

#     numbers mixed
# 1      1    1a
# 2      2    2b
```

```
# 3      3     3c

# 4      4     4d

# 5      5     5e


# subset rows using a logical condition

df6 = df[df$numbers < 10, keep_vars]

df6

#      numbers mixed

# 1      1     1a

# 2      2     2b

# 3      3     3c

# 4      4     4d

# 5      5     5e

# 6      6     6f

# 7      7     7g

# 8      8     8h

# 9      9     9i
```

SQL Introduction

Structured Query Language is one common language that is used in the retrieval of data from any kind of database. To demonstrate some basic SQL code, we are going to look at some examples. To focus on the language, we are going to look at SQL in R. when it comes to writing the code; it is the same as it is done in any database.

Three statements are in SQL: FROM, WHERE and SELECT. The most common cases of SQL code are utilized in the examples below. Go to the folder **bda/part2/SQL_introduction** and open the file **SQL_introduction.Rproj**. Next, open script **01_select.R.**to be able to write the SQL code in R, install**sqldf** package as follows

```r
# Install the sqldf package
install.packages('sqldf')


# load the library
library('sqldf')
library(nycflights13)


# We will be working with the fligths dataset in order to introduce SQL


# Let's take a look at the table
str(flights)
# Classes 'tbl_d', 'tbl' and 'data.frame':   336776 obs. of  16 variables:
# $ year     : int  2013 2013 2013 2013 2013 2013 2013 2013 2013 2013 ...
# $ month    : int  1 1 1 1 1 1 1 1 1 1 ...
# $ day      : int  1 1 1 1 1 1 1 1 1 1 ...
# $ dep_time : int  517 533 542 544 554 554 555 557 557 558 ...
# $ dep_delay: num  2 4 2 -1 -6 -4 -5 -3 -3 -2 ...
# $ arr_time : int  830 850 923 1004 812 740 913 709 838 753 ...
# $ arr_delay: num  11 20 33 -18 -25 12 19 -14 -8 8 ...
```

Data Analytics for Beginners

```
# $ carrier  : chr  "UA" "UA" "AA" "B6" ...
# $ tailnum  : chr  "N14228" "N24211" "N619AA" "N804JB" ...
# $ flight   : int  1545 1714 1141 725 461 1696 507 5708 79 301 ...
# $ origin   : chr  "EWR" "LGA" "JFK" "JFK" ...
# $ dest     : chr  "IAH" "IAH" "MIA" "BQN" ...
# $ air_time : num  227 227 160 183 116 150 158 53 140 138 ...
# $ distance : num  1400 1416 1089 1576 762 ...
# $ hour     : num  5 5 5 5 5 5 5 5 5 5 ...
# $ minute   : num  17 33 42 44 54 54 55 57 57 58 ...
```

Extraction of information that is in columns and calculation of this information from tables is done using the select statement. **ej1** demonstrates the simplest SELECT statement. New variables can be created in **ej2.**

```
### SELECT statement
ej1 = sqldf("
  SELECT
    dep_time
    ,dep_delay
    ,arr_time
    ,carrier
    ,tailnum
  FROM
    flights")


head(ej1)
#    dep_time  dep_delay  arr_time  carrier  tailnum
# 1     517        2        830      UA      N14228
# 2     533        4        850      UA      N24211
# 3     542        2        923      AA      N619AA
```

```
# 4      544      -1    1004   B6   N804JB
# 5      554      -6     812   DL   N668DN
# 6      554      -4     740   UA   N39463


# In R we can use SQL with the sqldf function. It works exactly the same as in a database

# The data.frame (in this case flights) represents the table we are querying and goes in the FROM statement

# We can also compute new variables in the select statement using the syntax:

# old_variables as new_variable

ej2 = sqldf("
  SELECT
    arr_delay - dep_delay as gain,
    carrier
  FROM
    flights")


ej2[1:5, ]
#     gain  carrier
# 1    9    UA
# 2   16    UA
# 3   31    AA
# 4  -17    B6
# 5  -19    DL
```

Group by statement is one of the common SQL features. It allows the computation of a numeric value for groups of other variables. Script **02_group_by.R** needs to be opened.

```
### GROUP BY


# Computing the average
ej3 = sqldf("
  SELECT
    avg(arr_delay) as mean_arr_delay,
    avg(dep_delay) as mean_dep_delay,
    carrier
  FROM
    flights
  GROUP BY
    carrier
")

#    mean_arr_delay mean_dep_delay carrier
# 1       7.3796692      16.725769      9E
# 2       0.3642909       8.586016      AA
# 3      -9.9308886       5.804775      AS
# 4       9.4579733      13.022522      B6
# 5       1.6443409       9.264505      DL
# 6      15.7964311      19.955390      EV
# 7      21.9207048      20.215543      F9
# 8      20.1159055      18.726075      FL
# 9      -6.9152047       4.900585      HA
# 10     10.7747334      10.552041      MQ
```

```
# 11      11.9310345    12.586207     OO
# 12       3.5580111    12.106073     UA
# 13       2.1295951     3.782418     US
# 14       1.7644644    12.869421     VX
# 15       9.6491199    17.711744     WN
# 16      15.5569853    18.996330     YV


# Other aggregations
ej4 = sqldf("
  SELECT
   avg(arr_delay) as mean_arr_delay,
   min(dep_delay) as min_dep_delay,
   max(dep_delay) as max_dep_delay,
   carrier
  FROM
    flights
  GROUP BY
    carrier
")

# We can compute the minimun, mean, and maximum values of a numeric value
ej4
#     mean_arr_delay   min_dep_delay   max_dep_delay   carrier
# 1      7.3796692         -24             747           9E
# 2      0.3642909         -24            1014           AA
# 3     -9.9308886         -21             225           AS
# 4      9.4579733         -43             502           B6
```

# 5	1.6443409	-33	960	DL
# 6	15.7964311	-32	548	EV
# 7	21.9207048	-27	853	F9
# 8	20.1159055	-22	602	FL
# 9	-6.9152047	-16	1301	HA
# 10	10.7747334	-26	1137	MQ
# 11	11.9310345	-14	154	OO
# 12	3.5580111	-20	483	UA
# 13	2.1295951	-19	500	US
# 14	1.7644644	-20	653	VX
# 15	9.6491199	-13	471	WN
# 16	15.5569853	-16	387	YV

We could be also interested in knowing how many observations each carrier has

```
ej5 = sqldf("
  SELECT
  carrier, count(*) as count
  FROM
    flights
  GROUP BY
    carrier
")

ej5
#     carrier  count
# 1      9E    18460
```

```
# 2      AA  32729
# 3      AS  714
# 4      B6  54635
# 5      DL  48110
# 6      EV  54173
# 7      F9  685
# 8      FL  3260
# 9      HA  342
# 10     MQ  26397
# 11     OO  32
# 12     UA  58665
# 13     US  20536
# 14     VX  5162
# 15     WN  12275
# 16     YV  601
```

Joins are the most useful features of the SQL code. It means that you want to combine two tables A and B in a table using a column to match values that are in both tables. There are different joins, in practical terms, to get started these will be the useful ones: left outer join and inner join.

```
# Let's create two tables: A and B to demonstrate joins.

A = data.frame(c1=1:4, c2=letters[1:4])

B = data.frame(c1=c(2,4,5,6), c2=letters[c(2:5)])


A

# c1 c2

# 1  a

# 2  b

# 3  c
```

```
# 4  d

B
# c1 c2
# 2  b
# 4  c
# 5  d
# 6  e


### INNER JOIN
# This means to match the observations of the column we would join the tables by.

inner = sqldf("
  SELECT
    A.c1, B.c2
  FROM
    A INNER JOIN B
    ON A.c1 = B.c1
")

# Only the rows that match c1 in both A and B are returned
inner
# c1 c2
#  2  b
#  4  c


### LEFT OUTER JOIN
```

```
# the left outer join, sometimes just called left join will return the
# first all the values of the column used from the A table

left = sqldf("
  SELECT
    A.c1, B.c2
  FROM
    A LEFT OUTER JOIN B
    ON A.c1 = B.c1
")

# Only the rows that match c1 in both A and B are returned
left
#   c1   c2
#   1   <NA>
#   2    b
#   3   <NA>
#   4    c
```

Graphs and Charts

Analyzing data is done efficiently when it is visualized. The main goal of visualizing is in finding the relations between variable descriptions that are univariate and variables. These strategies can be divided into two

- Multivariate analysis

- Univariate analysis

Data Analytics for Beginners

Univariate Analysis

This is a term in statistics that means to analyze a variable separately from all the other data. Plots that allow this kind of analysis include

Box Plots

These plots are common in distribution comparison. It is a great way to respect differences in distributions in a visual manner. It is possible to see differences between different prices of diamonds.

.

```
# We will be using the ggplot2 library for plotting
library(ggplot2)


data("diamonds")


# We will be using the diamonds dataset to analyze distributions of numeric
variables
head(diamonds)
#   carat       cut   color clarity depth table price    x    y    z
# 1  0.23     Ideal   E     SI2     61.5   55   326   3.95 3.98 2.43
# 2  0.21   Premium   E     SI1     59.8   61   326   3.89 3.84 2.31
# 3  0.23      Good   E     VS1     56.9   65   327   4.05 4.07 2.31
# 4  0.29   Premium   I     VS2     62.4   58   334   4.20 4.23 2.63
# 5  0.31      Good   J     SI2     63.3   58   335   4.34 4.35 2.75
# 6  0.24 Very Good   J     VVS2    62.8   57   336   3.94 3.96 2.48
### Box-Plots
```

```
p = ggplot(diamonds, aes(x=cut, y=price, fill=cut)) +
  geom_box-plot() +
  theme_bw()
print(p)
```

Differences can be seen in the plot of the distribution of prices of diamond is in different kinds of cut.

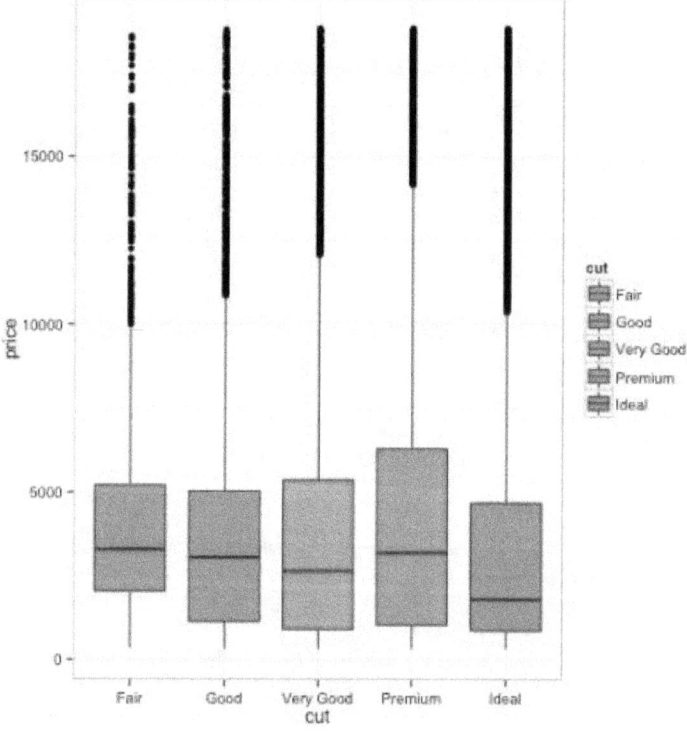

This is a box plot that compares numeric variable distribution among a variable factor

Histograms

```
source('01_box_plots.R')


# We can plot histograms for each level of the cut factor variable using
facet_grid

p = ggplot(diamonds, aes(x=price, fill=cut)) +

  geom_histogram() +

  facet_grid(cut ~ .) +

  theme_bw()

p


# the previous plot doesn't allow to visuallize correctly the data because of
the differences in scale

# we can turn this off using the scales argument of facet_grid


p = ggplot(diamonds, aes(x=price, fill=cut)) +

  geom_histogram() +

  facet_grid(cut ~ ., scales='free') +

  theme_bw()

p


png('02_histogram_diamonds_cut.png')

print(p)

dev.off()
```

The output is as shown below

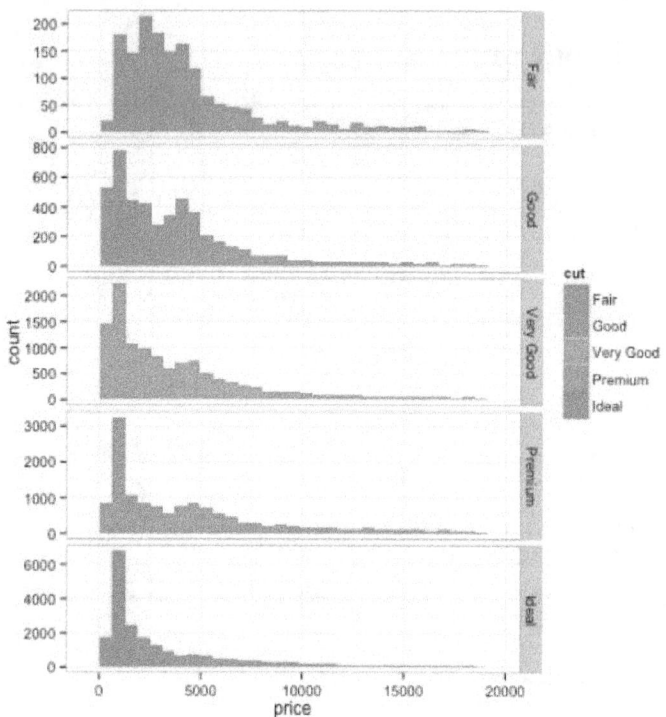

Multivariate Analysis

This type of graphical method is used in exploratory analysis of data has the goal of discovering the relationships between variables that are different. There are two ways where this can be done; one is the plotting of a matrix correlation of variables that are numeric or plotting raw data of scatter plots matrix.

To demonstrate this, the diamond data set is used. You can open the script below to follow the code

Bda.part2/charts/03_multivariate_analysis.R

```
library(ggplot2)
data(diamonds)
# Correlation matrix plots


keep_vars = c('carat', 'depth', 'price', 'table')
df = diamonds[, keep_vars]


# compute the correlation matrix
M_cor = cor(df)
#          carat       depth      price      table
# carat 1.00000000  0.02822431  0.9215913  0.1816175
# depth 0.02822431  1.00000000 -0.0106474 -0.2957785
# price 0.92159130 -0.01064740  1.0000000  0.1271339
# table 0.18161755 -0.29577852  0.1271339  1.0000000


# plots
heat-map(M_cor)
```

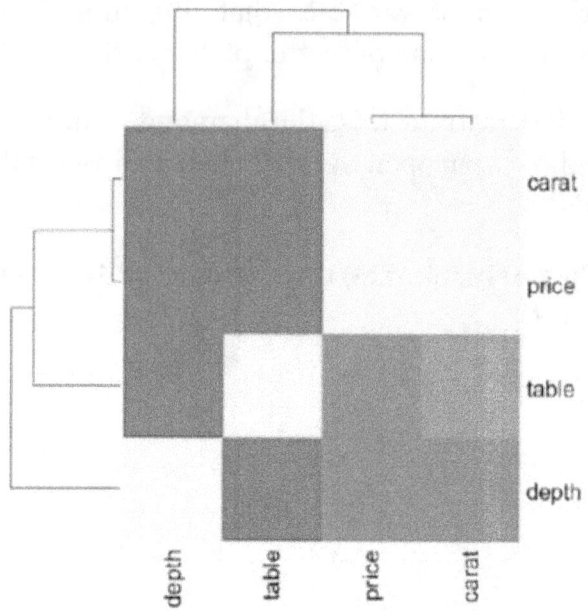

The following output will be produced

Corrclation Matrix Hcat Map

This heat map is a summary that says there is a correlation that is strong between caret and price, and less in other variables.

The correlation matrix is useful with large variables were plotting raw data is not practical.

Data Analytics for Beginners

As we indicated, showing the raw data is also possible.

```
library(GGally)
ggpairs(df)
```

The results displayed in the heat map are confirmed, a correlation of 0.922 between carat variables and price.

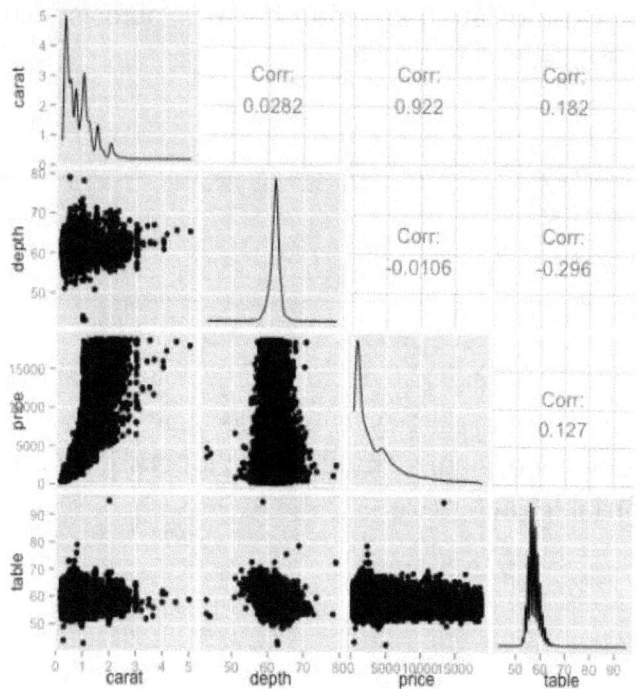

This is a scatter plot matrix of variables that are numeric from the dataset of diamonds

Data Analysis Tools

There are several types of tools that can perform data analysis efficiently. Data scientists focus on tools that can implement data products. The section we are getting into showcases the different tools as we focus on the packages that data scientist uses often.

Data Analytics for Beginners

R Programming

This is an open source language that programs with a focus on statistical analysis. Its main competitors include SPSS and SAS. It can be an interface to languages such as C++ or C or Fortran.

One advantage of R is the sheer number of libraries it had. There are over 600 packages in CRAN that care downloadable. There is also a wide range of R packages on Github.

Looking at performance, R is slower because of its operations which are intense, given the libraries that are huge, the sections of the code that are slow are in compiled languages. If you plan to write for loops that are deep, R would not be the ideal option. For the purpose of data analysis, nice libraries exist like **data.table, ranger, glmnet, caret, ggplot2, xgboost**which allow R usage as a faster language interface.

Data Analysis using Python

Python is a programming language that is used in many applications, and it has quite a number of libraries that are made for data analysis. These include scikit-learn, pandas, numpy ,scipy, and theano.

Most of the functionalities that R have can be done in Python, even though R is way simpler in use. When working with large data sets, Python is preferred than R. It is effective to clean and process data; R can manage, but it is not that efficient when you compare it to Python when it comes to scripting tasks.

When it comes to machine learning, scikit-learn is an environment that has algorithms that are available to handle medium-sized datasets easily. Scikit-learn has a cleaner and consistent API compared to R's library.

Julia

This is a high-level dynamic programming language that is used for computing. It has a similar syntax to Python or R, so if you have Python and R, you should have it easy when writing in Julia. It is a new language that has grown over the years.

Julia is recommended to algorithmic prototyping which is computationally intensive like neural networks; it is great in research. When it comes to implementing a production module, Python is a great alternative. Currently, this selection issue has become outdated since the emergence of web services that have Julia, Python and R models implemented.

SAS

This is a commercial or industrial language used mostly for business intelligence. Its base language allows the users to come up with various kinds of applications. It has a couple of commercial products that provide non-experts the ability to use complex tools like a library of a neural network without programming.

Beyond commercial tools disadvantages, SAS is not scalable to datasets. It will have a problem with medium-sized datasets as it will make the server slow down and crash. If you are working on small datasets, and the users are not data scientists, then SAS is the best option. Python and R are for advanced users.

SPSS

This is a product of IBM. It is used mostly to analyze survey data and users who cannot program. It is simple to use, just like SAS, but when it comes to modeling, it is easy to use because it provides the SQL code for scoring a model. The code is not usually efficient, but it is a step whereas SAS sells the product that scores models separately for different databases. SPS is a good option for small data sets and a team that is not experienced. The software is limited, and users who are experienced will be productive in Python or R compared to SPSS.

Octave, Matlab

Matlab and its Octave version that is open source are tools available to the public. Python or R can do all that Octave or Matlab can do. When you want to purchase these options, the only option that makes sense in purchasing them as if one is looking for the support that they are providing

Chapter 7: Statistical Methods of Big Data Analytics

In data analysis, the basic tools that are needed for basic analysis are

- Correlation
- Analysis variance
- Hypothesis testing

When large data sets are being worked on, a problem is not involved as the methods are not intensive computationally except for analysis correlation.

Correlation analysis

This seeks to find linear relationships that exist between variables that are numeric. Different circumstances can use this; one common use is the data analysis that is exploratory. First of all, the correlation metric used in the example is dependent on Pearson coefficient. It is another correlation metric that outliers do not affect. This is called a Spearman correlation metric. It is robust when outliers are presented compared to the Pearson coefficient method. The Spearman method has better estimates of relations that are linear between variables numerals when there is a normal distribution of data.

```r
library(ggplot2)


# Select variables that are interesting to compare pearson and spearman
correlation methods.

x = diamonds[, c('x', 'y', 'z', 'price')]


# From the histograms we can expect differences in the correlations of both
metrics.

# In this case as the variables are clearly not normally distributed, the
spearman correlation

# is a better estimate of the linear relation among numeric variables.

par(mfrow=c(2,2))

colnm = names(x)

for(i in 1:4){
```

```r
  hist(x[[i]], col='deepskyblue3', main=sprintf('Histogram of %s', colnm[i]))

}

par(mfrow=c(1,1))
```

When you look at histograms in the figure below differences are expected in correlations that are in both metrics. Since there is no clear normal distribution of variables in the case below,

Spearman correlation is better at estimating linear relations in variables that are numeric.

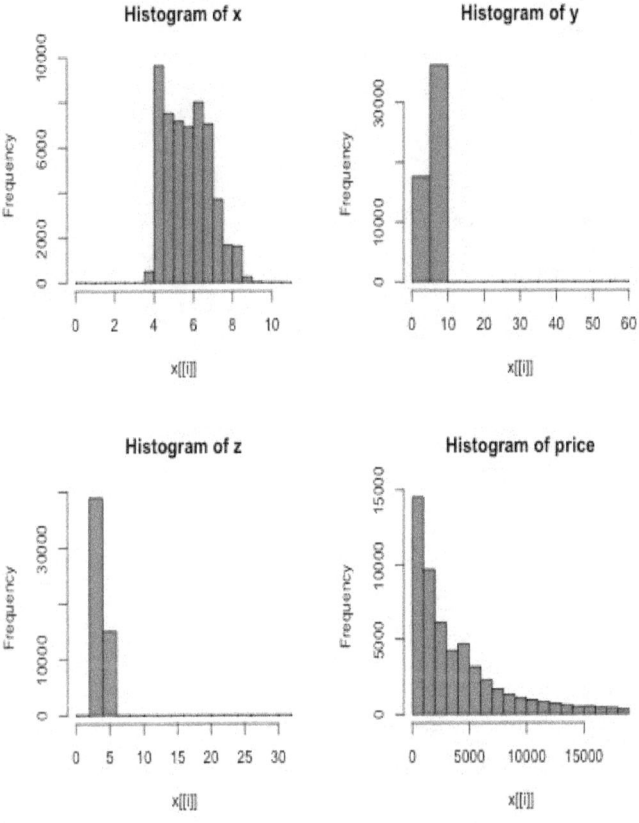

The diagram above is a non-normally distributed histogram

To compute correlation in R, the file **bda/part2/statistical_methods/correlati**

on/correlation.R needs to be open which has a code section.

```
## Correlation Matrix - Pearson and spearman
cor_pearson <- cor(x, method='pearson')
cor_spearman <- cor(x, method='spearman')

### Pearson Correlation
print(cor_pearson)
#              x          y          z         price
# x      1.0000000  0.9747015  0.9707718  0.8844352
# y      0.9747015  1.0000000  0.9520057  0.8654209
# z      0.9707718  0.9520057  1.0000000  0.8612494
# price  0.8844352  0.8654209  0.8612494  1.0000000


### Spearman Correlation
print(cor_spearman)
#              x          y          z         price
# x      1.0000000  0.9978949  0.9873553  0.9631961
# y      0.9978949  1.0000000  0.9870675  0.9627188
# z      0.9873553  0.9870675  1.0000000  0.9572323
# price  0.9631961  0.9627188  0.9572323  1.0000000
```

T-Test

Evaluation of the differences in numerical variable distribution is what this test is about. The differences in distribution are between groups that are a variable that is nominal. T-tests are implemented using t.test function in R. the interface formula to t.test is explained by a group variable. For instance, t.test(numeric_variable ~ group_variable, data=data).

Conclusion

Thank for making it through to the end of ***Data Analytics for Beginners:*** *A Beginner's Guide to Learn and Master Data Analytics*, let's hope it was informative and able to provide you with all of the tools you need to handle the data that your business collects every day, to make better business decisions. Just because you have finished this book does not mean there is nothing left to learn on the topic, expanding your horizons is the only way to take advantage of the insights that are within your business data

The next step is to stop reading and to start using the different tools that have been suggested in this book to see if they are useful in your company. Always ensure that you consult your data analyst for the best tools to use in case you want more advanced tools to process your complex data. If you find that you have very simple data, you can download the tools we have recommended and use them in step by step manner.

Studies show that complex data that are produced through all interactive systems like the social media platforms need to be understood by intelligent systems that are more advanced than the tools we have shown. Other books dig deeper into complex data analysis tools for advanced data analysis; go ahead and consult business intelligence experts on some of these tools which are licensed for them to be used.

Finally, if you found this book useful in anyway, a review on Amazon is always appreciated!

www.ingramcontent.com/pod-product-compliance
Lightning Source LLC
Chambersburg PA
CBHW070303230526
45470CB00002B/697